FAMOUS JOURNEYS

ANNA NILSEN

How to do the puzzles

On your voyage of discovery around the world, you will encounter three different types of puzzles—all designed to challenge your observational skills!

Great Explorer Mazes

There are four great explorer mazes to test your abilities as a navigator. Begin by looking for a green flag and a red flag. The green flag is your starting point. From here, make your way through the maze until you reach your final destination: the red flag.

Spot the Difference

Four explorers have set you a tricky task. You will find two identical scenes to compare—but are they really identical? Look again! The right-hand scene contains ten objects which don't belong. Can you find them?

Spotter puzzles

You'll need eagle eyes to do the spotter puzzles!

Mini-mazes

The first two spotter discs show the start and finish of a 'mini-maze'. How quickly can you find your way between them?

Hunt-and-find

The explorers have also been busy counting and studying the wildlife in the places they visited. There are ten 'spotter discs'—four show a creature **(A)**, four show a small detail **(B)** of a creature, and two show only the silhouette **(C)** of a creature. Carefully count how many you find of each creature in the discs and write down your answers as you go. You should be able to put the answers in order from one to ten. That is, you should find one creature to match one disc, two creatures for another disc, and so on up to ten. If you have duplicates of any number, count again. You should find 55 creatures in total.

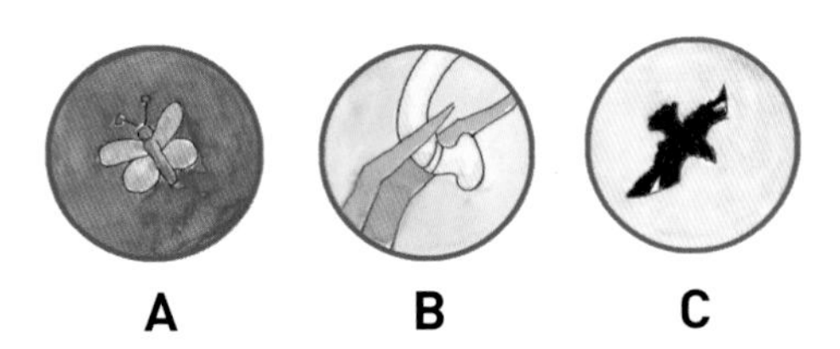

Twelve incredible journeys—twelve challenging puzzles!

You are about to embark on a great adventure, one which will take you through time—and even space!—as you follow in the footsteps of twelve of the world's most famous adventurers. These daring men and women will lead you on fascinating journeys—across hazardous Arctic ice, over rugged mountains, down into treacherous ravines, through steamy African jungles, to the depths of the sea, and up into space. You can read more about their heroic deeds at the back of the book, straight after the last puzzle.

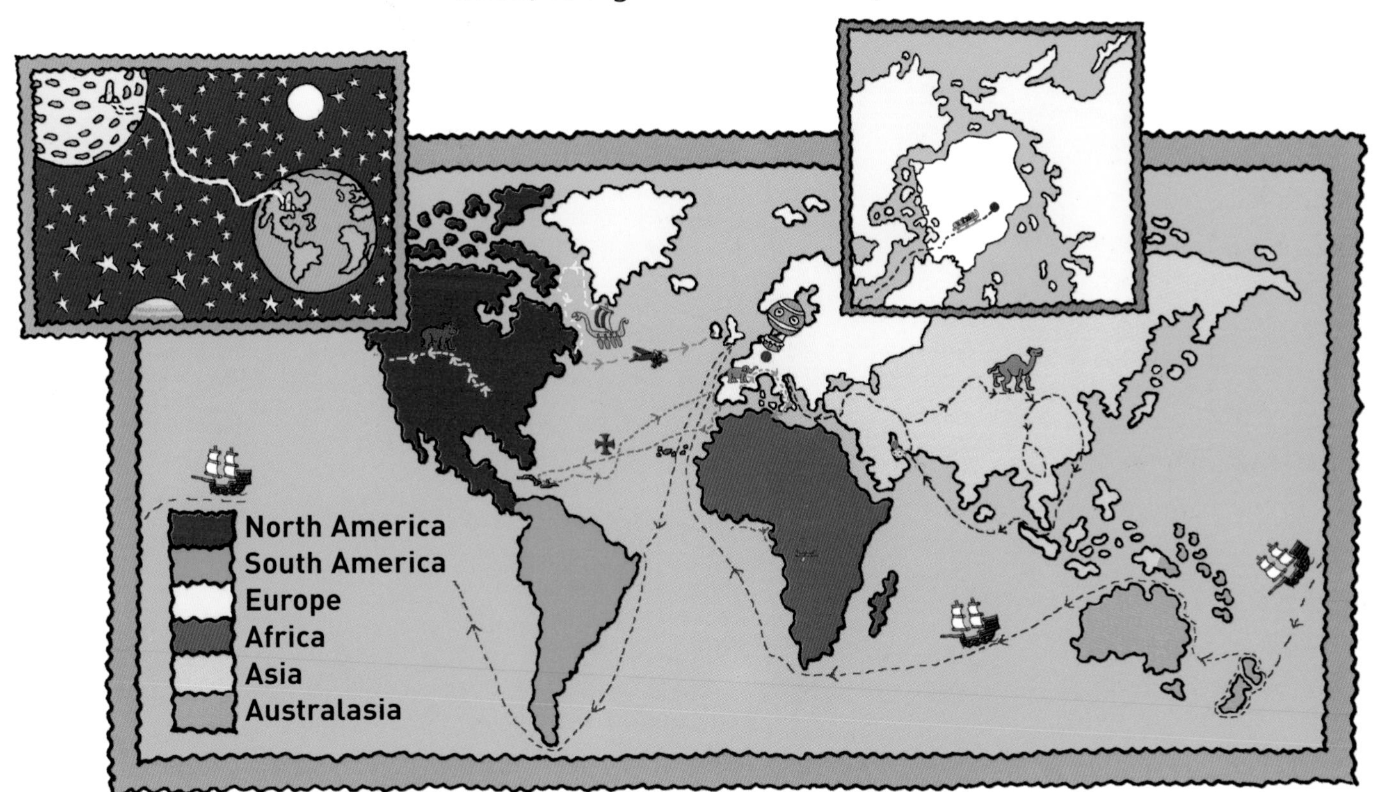

Hannibal
Trek across the Alps with Hannibal and his elephants in 218BC. Hurry, or you could be caught in a snowstorm!

Leif Erikson
Leif Erikson and his crew have been busy spotting mammals and birds in Newfoundland in 1001. Now it's your turn to find 55 creatures—and follow the mini-maze!
START
FINISH

Marco Polo
In 1275, Marco Polo visited the palace of the great emperor Kublai Khan. Can you spot ten differences between these two pictures?

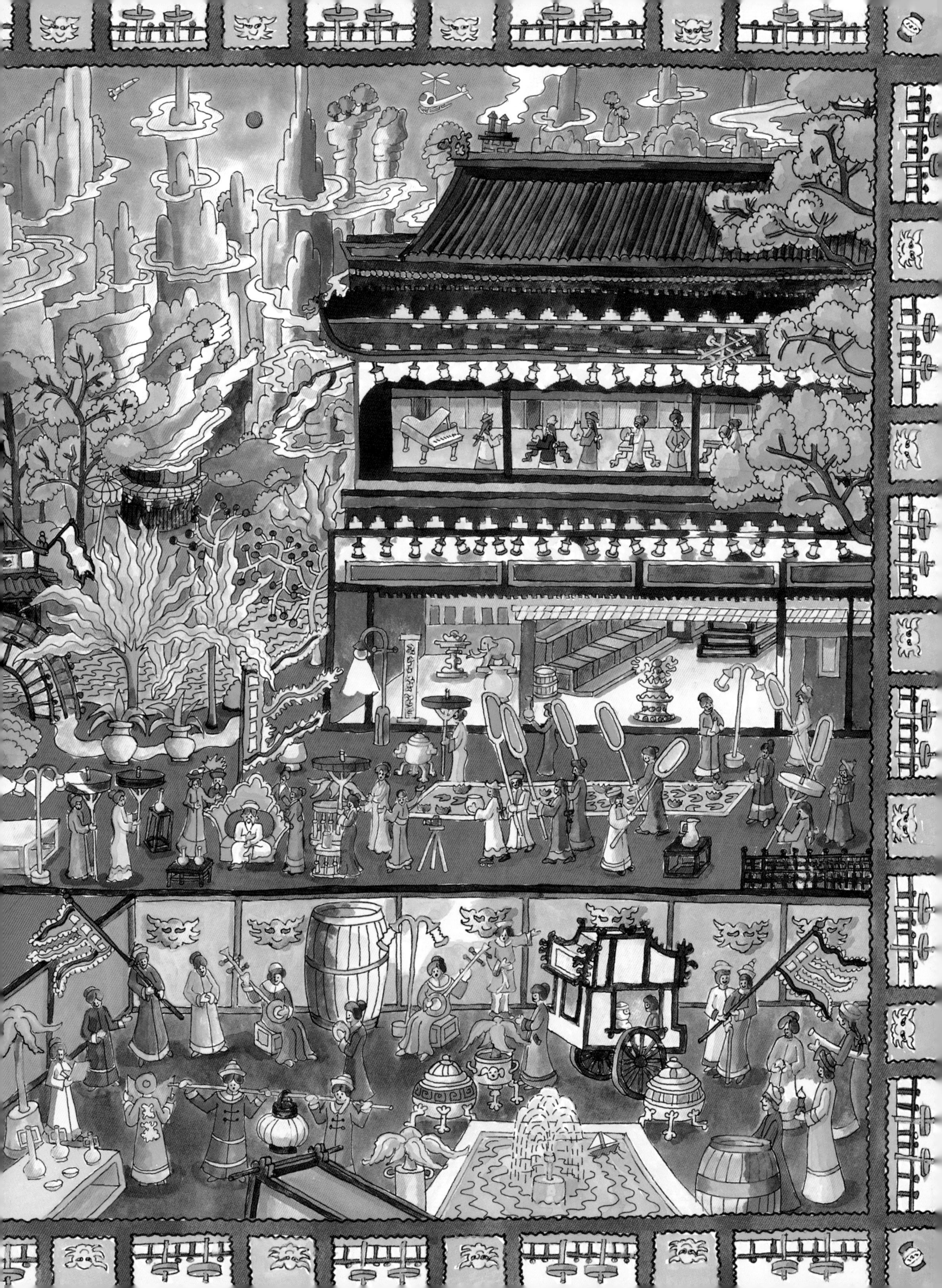

Christopher Columbus

In 1492 Christopher Columbus set out on his journey of discovery. Can you spot ten differences between these two pictures?

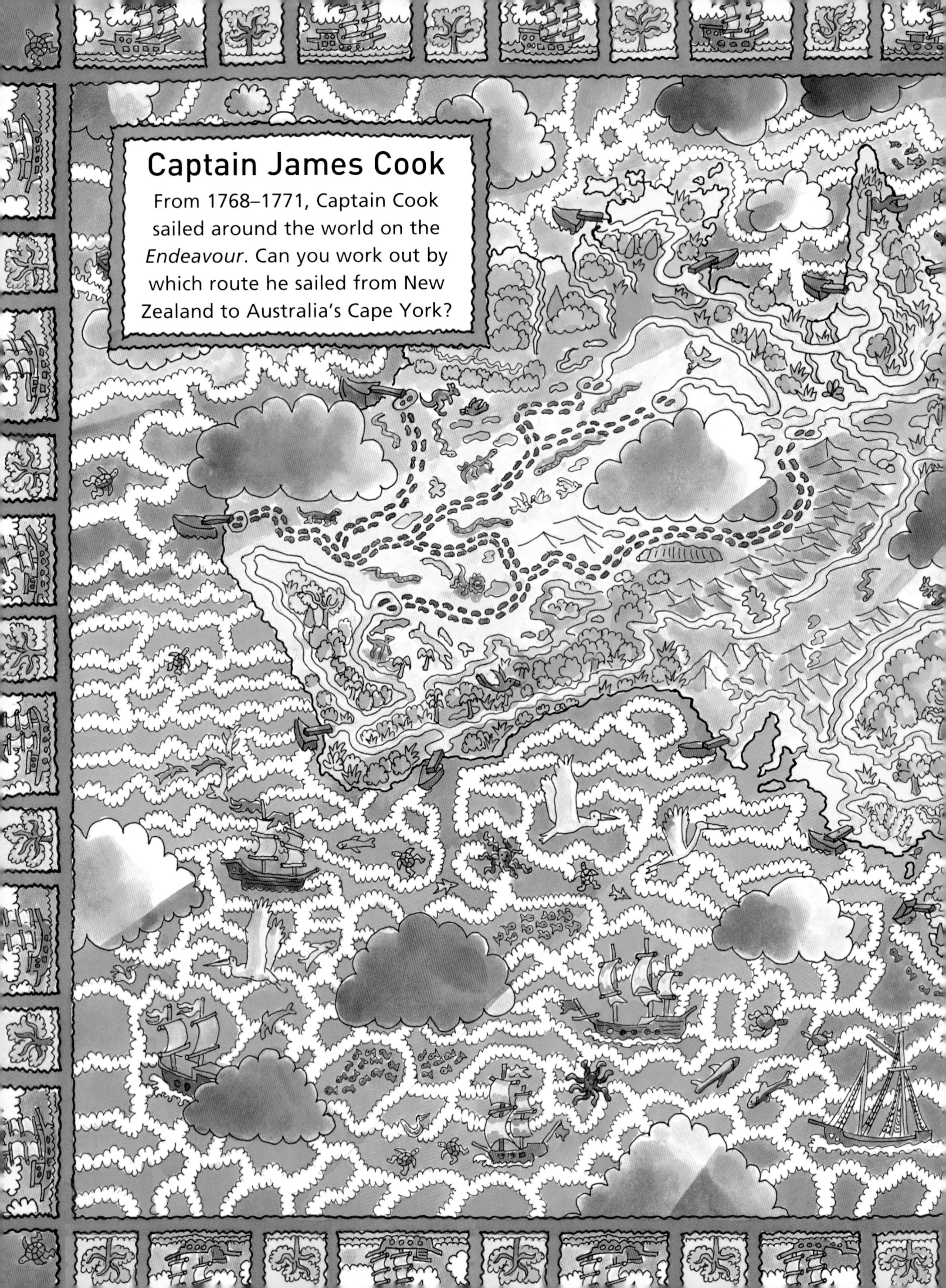
Captain James Cook
From 1768–1771, Captain Cook sailed around the world on the *Endeavour*. Can you work out by which route he sailed from New Zealand to Australia's Cape York?

The Montgolfiers
The Montgolfier brothers invented the hot-air balloon in 1783.
Can you spot ten differences between these two pictures?

Lewis and Clark
Navigate the rapids that Lewis and Clark encountered on their adventure through the rugged gorges of Snake River in 1805.

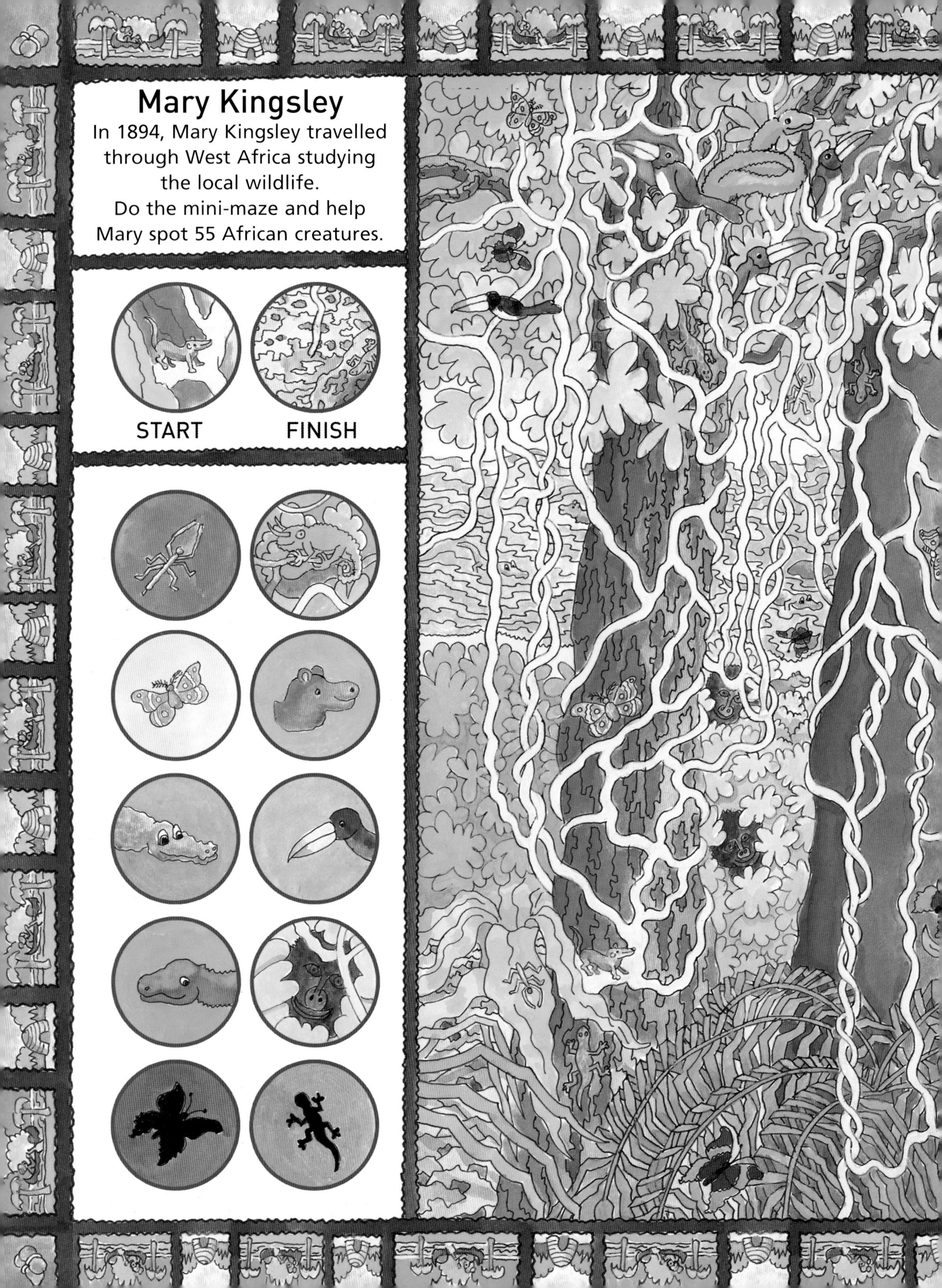
Mary Kingsley
In 1894, Mary Kingsley travelled through West Africa studying the local wildlife.
Do the mini-maze and help Mary spot 55 African creatures.
START
FINISH

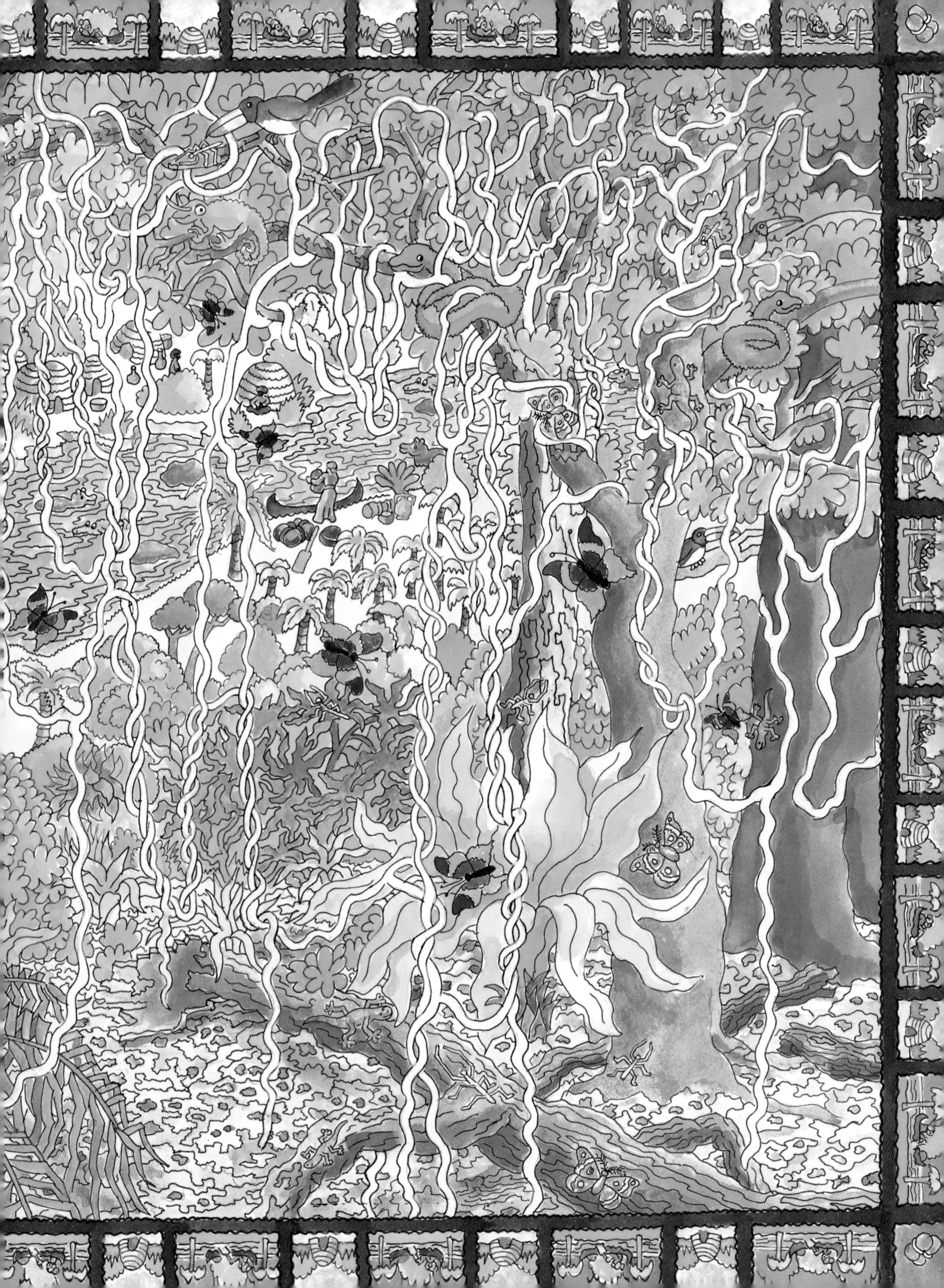

Peary and Henson
In 1909, Peary and Henson were the first people to reach the North Pole. Do the mini-maze and help them spot 55 Arctic creatures.
START
FINISH

Amelia Earhart

Amelia Earhart flew solo across the Atlantic Ocean in 1932. Can you spot ten differences between these two pictures?

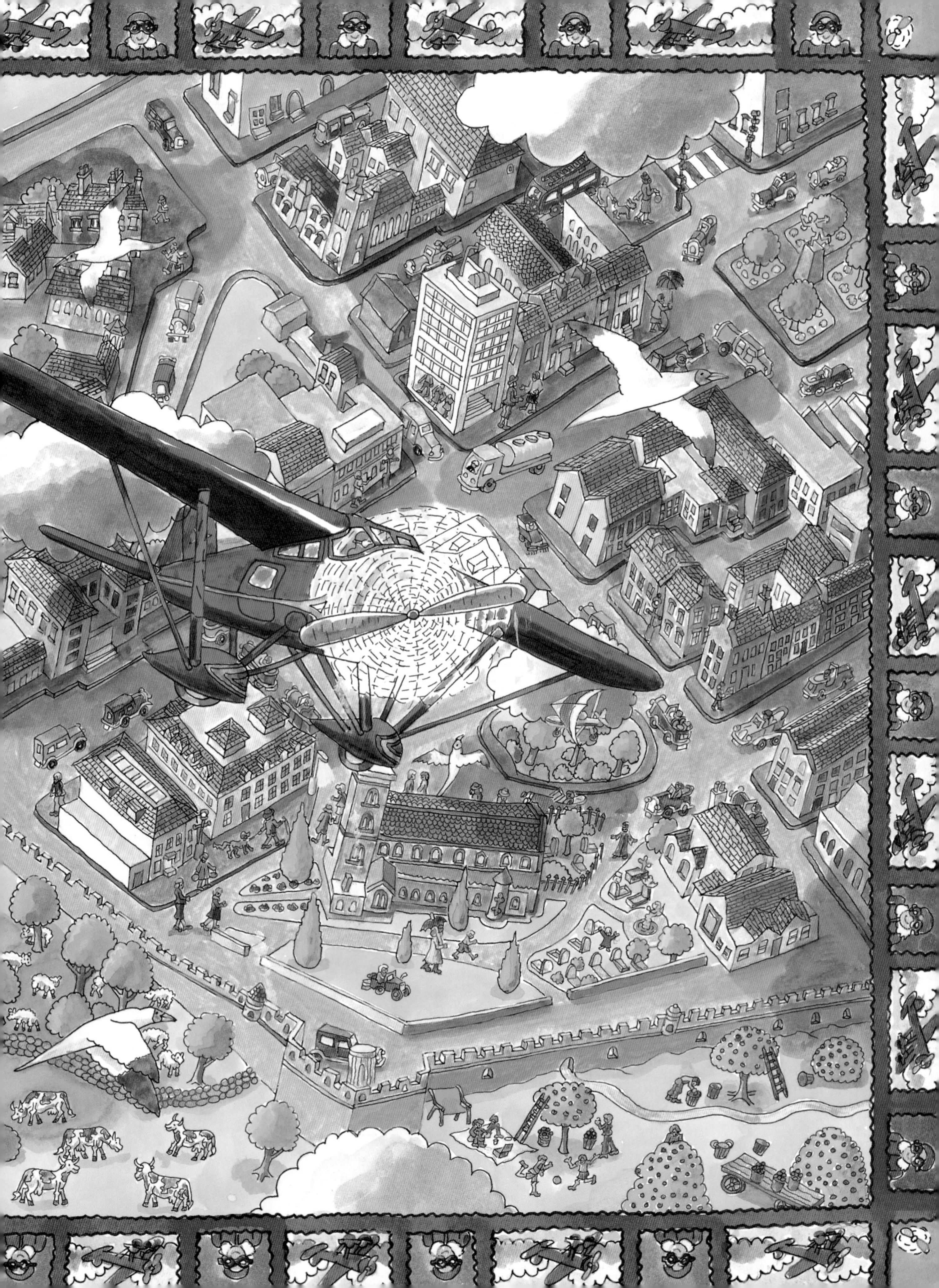

Jacques Cousteau
In 1963, Jacques Cousteau lived
beneath the Red Sea for four weeks
in an underwater diving bell.
Do the mini-maze and help
Cousteau spot 55 sea creatures.
START
FINISH

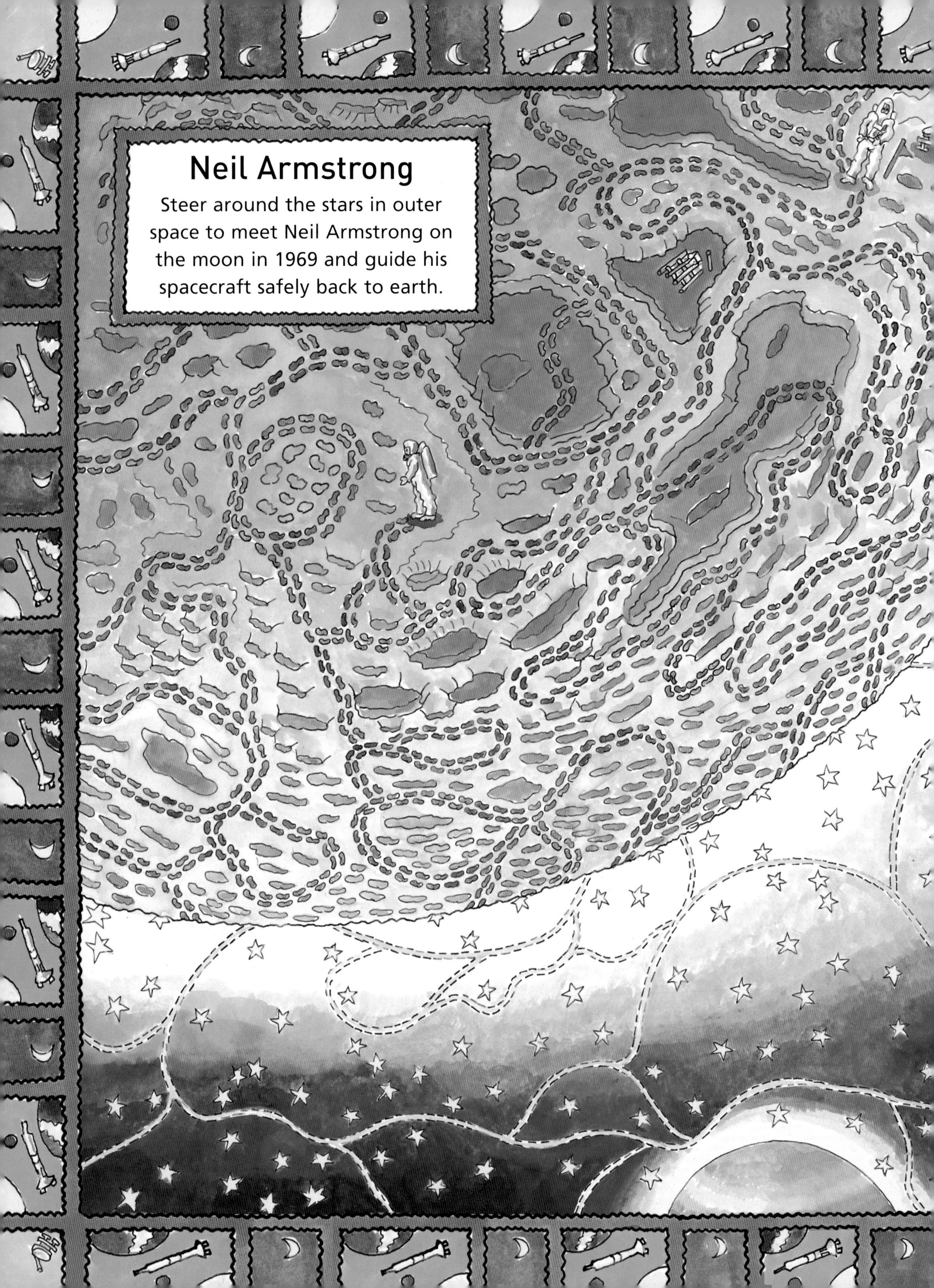

Neil Armstrong
Steer around the stars in outer space to meet Neil Armstrong on the moon in 1969 and guide his spacecraft safely back to earth.

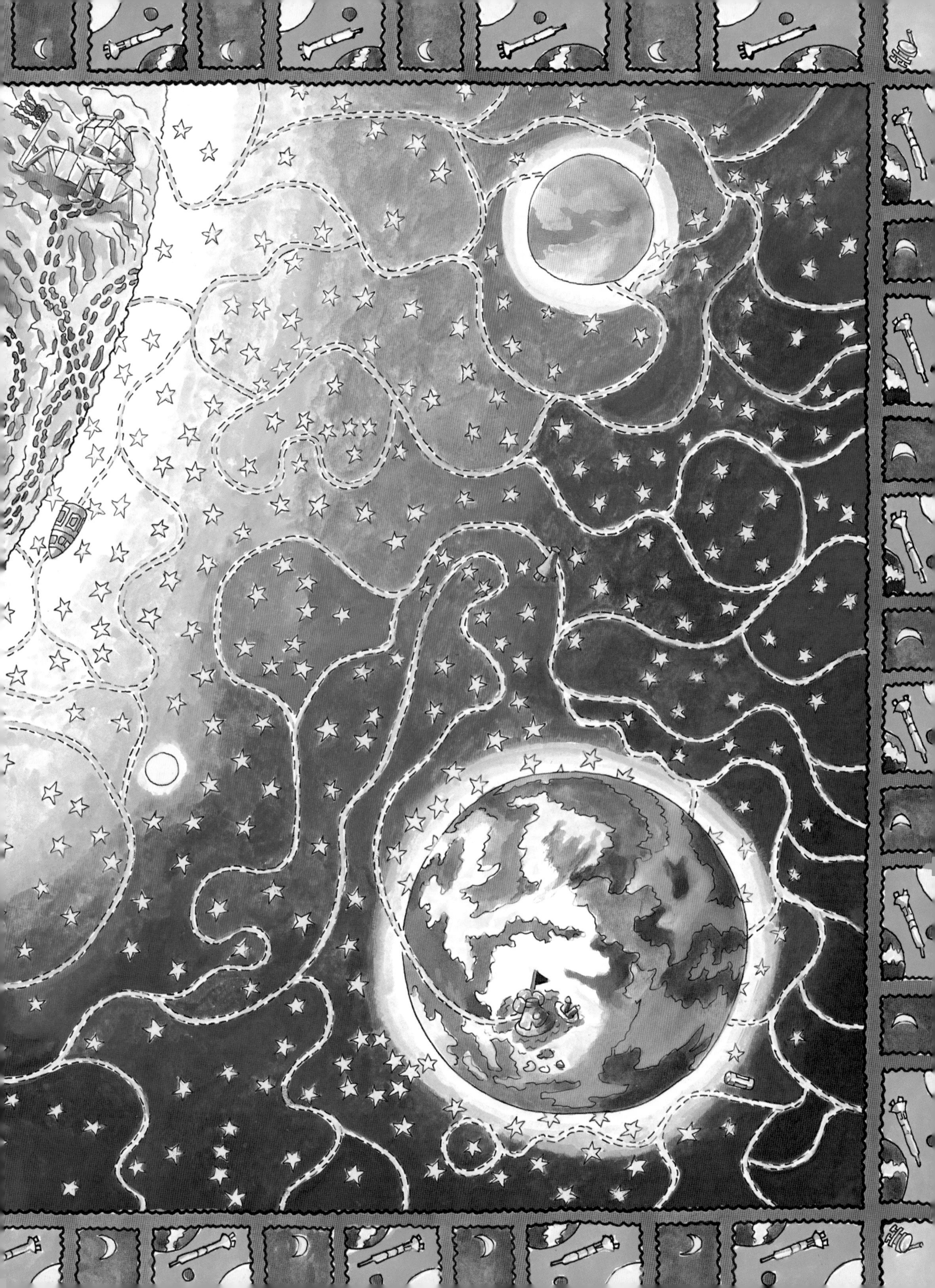

Hannibal

In 218BC, Hannibal—a military commander—led an army made up of infantry, cavalry and over thirty elephants on an epic five-month journey from Spain to Italy, crossing both the Pyrenees and the Alps. Only a few of the elephants survived the cold, arduous journey.

Leif Erikson

Leif Erikson, the son of Viking explorer Eric the Red, inherited his father's spirit of adventure. In 1001, Leif sailed west, ultimately landing in a place he called Vinland. It is now believed that this was somewhere between Cape Cod and Newfoundland, making Erikson the first European to set foot in North America.

Marco Polo

In 1271, Marco Polo set off from Venice with his father and uncle. They travelled for four years across mountains and deserts until they reached the palace of Kublai Khan in China. Marco, who could speak several languages, worked in the emperor's court for 15 years before returning home.

Christopher Columbus

Columbus was an Italian navigator employed by the king and queen of Spain to search for a direct trade route to Asia. He set off on his first voyage in 1492, sailing across the Atlantic and eventually landing on an island in the Bahamas. His voyages mark the beginning of European exploration and colonisation of the Americas.

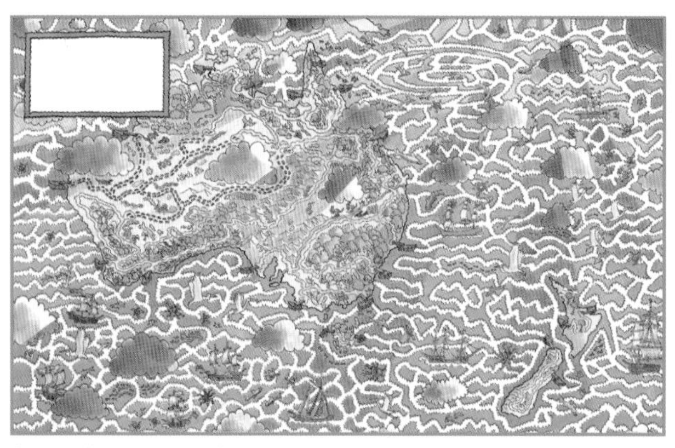

Captain James Cook

On three long journeys, British sea captain James Cook sailed to all seven continents, and was the first to cross the south polar circle. On his first voyage (1768-1771), aboard the *Endeavour*, he explored New Zealand and the Australian east coast.

The Montgolfier Brothers

French inventors Joseph and Jacques Montgolfier first launched a linen bag filled with hot air in June 1783. The first flight by humans took off from Paris in November. (Interestingly, only one of the brothers ever flew in a balloon himself—and he only did it once!)

Meriwether Lewis and William Clark

In 1804, with forty men—including botanists, zoologists and specialists in Native American sign language—Lewis and Clark set off up the Missouri River on an expedition of exploration. The two friends then trekked across North Dakota and Montana, and over the Continental Divide to the mouth of the Columbia River.

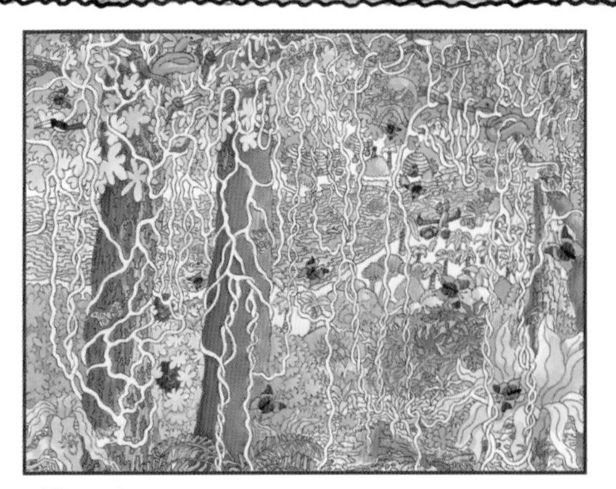

Mary Kingsley

British-born Mary Kingsley, the daughter of a doctor who travelled extensively, decided to travel to West Africa after her parents died in 1892. On her trips she collected specimens for the British Museum, and did much to advance the study of African customs, culture and wildlife.

Robert Peary and Matthew Henson

American Robert Peary made many trips to the Arctic region in preparation for his greatest ambition: to reach the North Pole. After several unsuccessful attempts, Peary and Matthew Henson, his associate, led a sledge party to the North Pole on 6 April 1909. Henson, an African American, reached the Pole first.

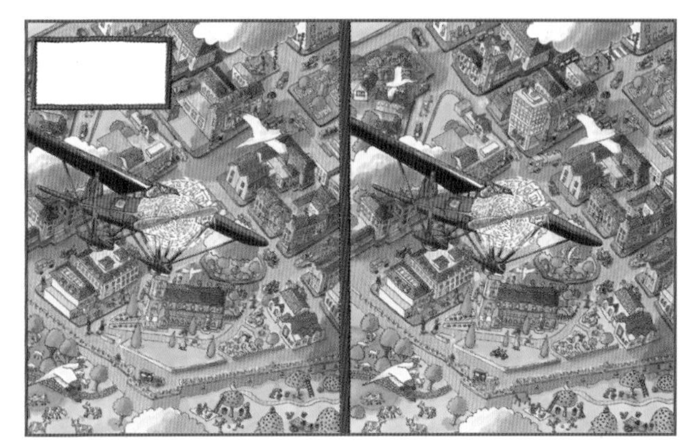

Amelia Earhart

In 1932, exactly five years after Charles Lindbergh's solo flight across the Atlantic, American aviatrix Amelia Earhart set off in her Lockheed Vega to become the first woman to make this crossing. She flew through storms, leaked petrol and nearly crashed into the sea, but eventually landed safely in an Irish field.

Jacques Cousteau

Twentieth-century oceanographer Jacques-Yves Cousteau, the French co-inventor of the aqualung, sailed the world on his ship *Calypso* to further his undersea explorations. His award-winning films, books and TV series introduced millions of people to the wonders of the ocean.

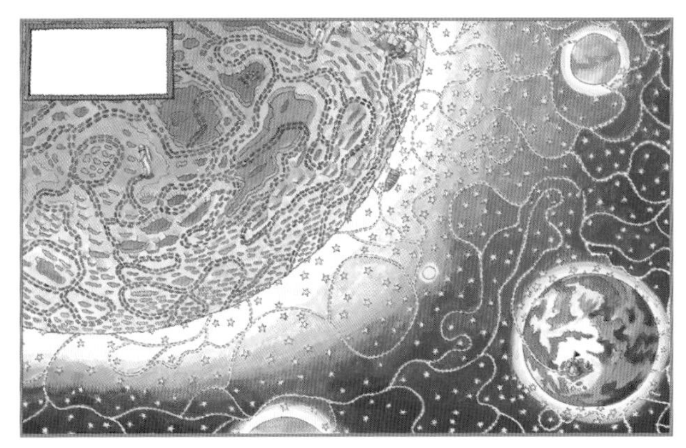

Neil Armstrong

American astronaut Neil Armstrong successfully performed the first docking in space in 1966. Three years later, as commander of *Apollo 11*, he and fellow astronaut Edwin 'Buzz' Aldrin landed on the moon, where Armstrong took the first steps on the moon's surface.

Solutions

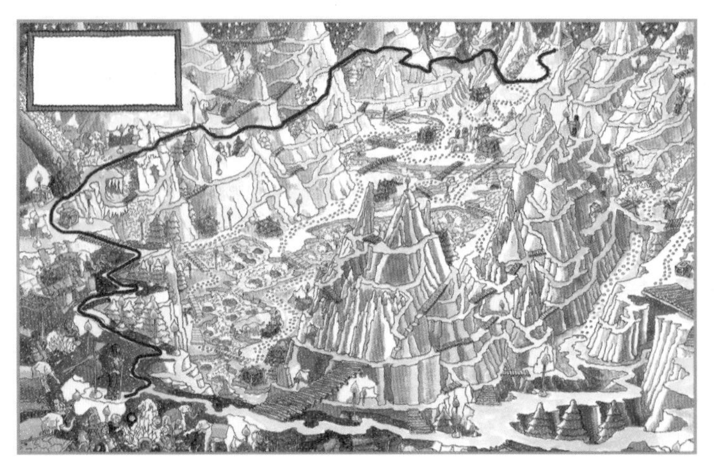

Hannibal

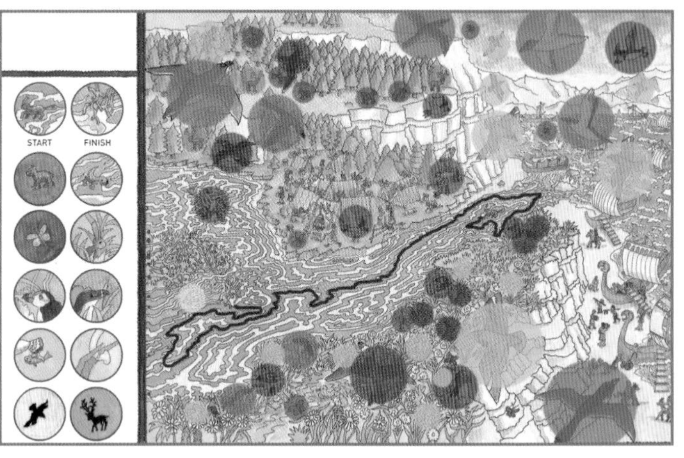

Leif Erikson

Marco Polo

Christopher Columbus

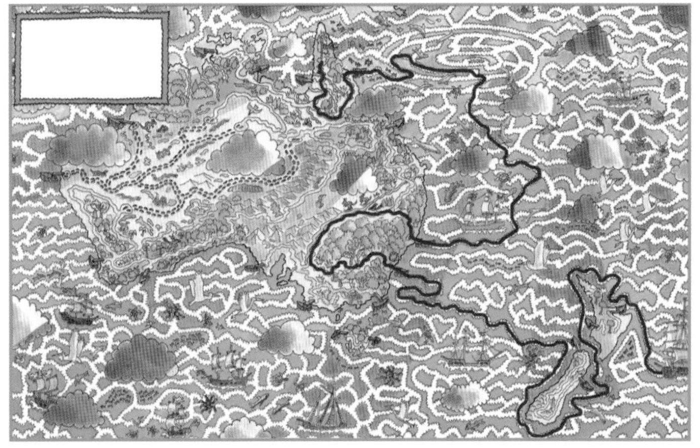

Captain James Cook

The Montgolfier Brothers

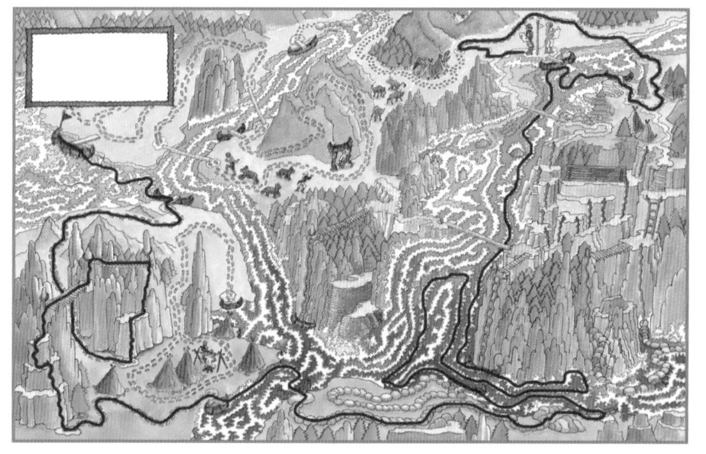

Meriwether Lewis and William Clark

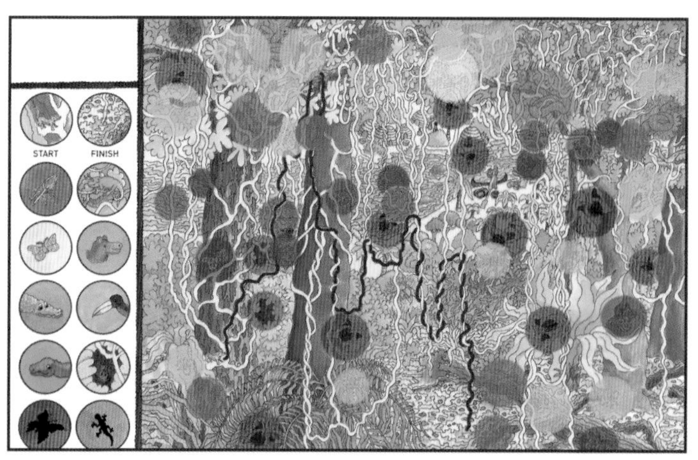

Mary Kingsley

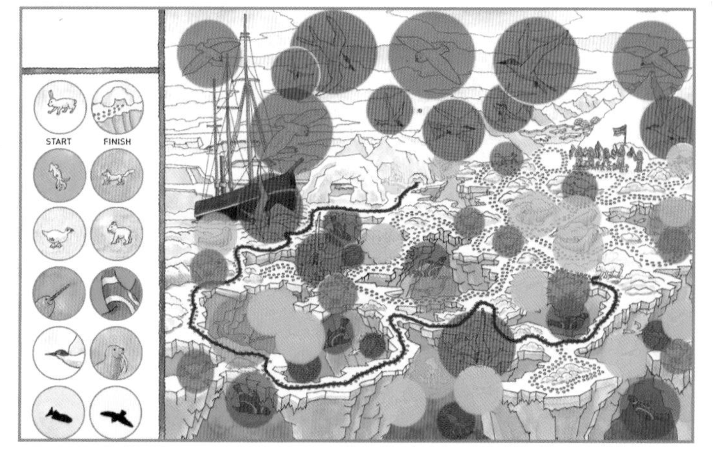

Robert Peary and Matthew Henson

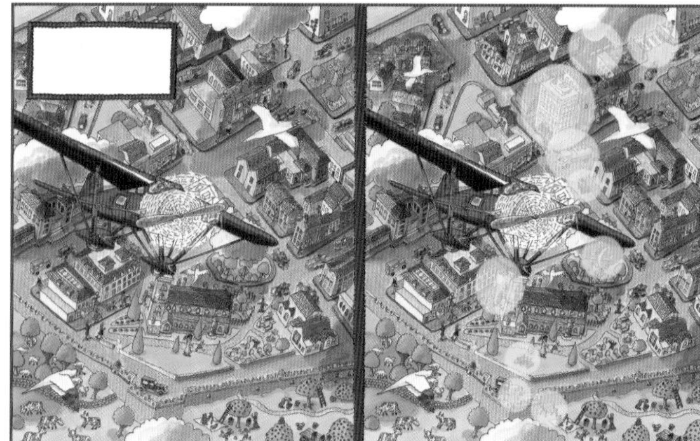

Amelia Earhart

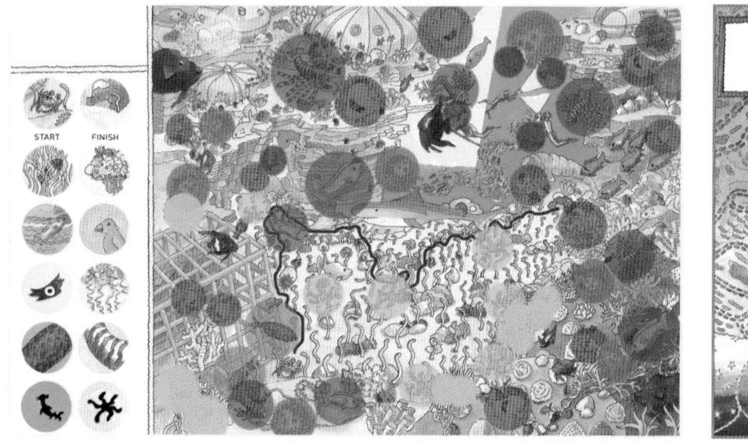

Jacques Cousteau

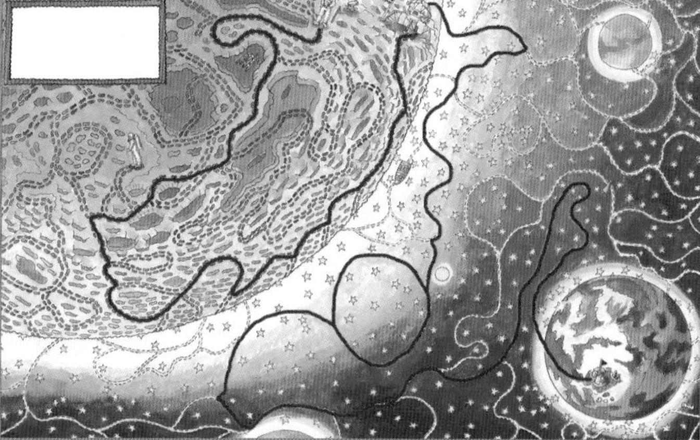

Neil Armstrong

To Blaze, Bumpers, Cass, Harvey, Hattie, Peter and Ulla
—From ATB and Tara

Little Hare Books
4/21 Mary Street, Surry Hills
NSW 2010 AUSTRALIA

www.littleharebooks.com

First published in 2005

National Library of Australia
Cataloguing-in-Publication entry

Nilsen, Anna.
Famous journeys.

For children.
ISBN 1 877003 88 3 (pbk.).

1. Picture puzzles – Juvenile literature. 2. Maze puzzles – Juvenile literature. 3. Explorers – Juvenile literature.
I. Title.

793.73

Designed by Serious Business
Produced by Phoenix Offset, Hong Kong
Printed in China

5 4 3 2 1